THE FRENCH LIEUTENANT'S WOMAN

NOTES

including
Life of the Author
Introduction
Critical Commentaries
Structure, Style, and Technique
List of Characters
Study Questions
Selected Bibliography

by
James F. Bellman, Jr.
and
Kathryn Bellman

consulting editor
James L. Roberts, Ph.D.
Department of English
University of Nebraska

INCORPORATED
LINCOLN, NEBRASKA   68501

ISBN 0-8220-0499-2

CONTENTS

Life of the Author

John Fowles was born in 1926 in Bedford, England. After graduation from Oxford University, where he studied French, he taught in France and also for several years on a Greek island, then returned to England and worked on his first novel, *The Collector,* published in 1963. After its publication, and the good reviews which it received, he gave up teaching to pursue writing full time.

Fowles' next work was *The Aristos,* a collection of philosophical aphorisms, published in 1965. *The Magus,* his next novel, was published in 1966, and in 1978 he published a revision of it. *The French Lieutenant's Woman* appeared in 1969. *The Ebony Tower,* a collection of short stories, was published in 1974, and his last novel to date, *Daniel Martin,* appeared in 1978.

John Fowles currently lives with his wife in Lyme Regis, Dorset, England.

Introduction

This novel is based on the nineteenth-century romantic or gothic novel, a literary genre which can trace its origins back to the eighteenth century. Although Fowles perfectly reproduces typical characters, situations, and even dialogue, the reader should always be aware of the irony inherent in Fowles' perception; for his perspective, however cleverly disguised, is that of the twentieth century. We see this both in the authorial intrusions, which comment on the mores of people in Victorian England, and in his choice of opening quotations, which are drawn from the writings of people whose observations belie the assumptions that most Victorians held about their world.

Fowles is concerned in this novel with the effects of society on the individual's awareness of himself or herself and how that awareness dominates and distorts his or her entire life, including relationships with other people. All the main characters in this novel are molded by what they believe to be true about themselves and others. In this case, their lives are governed by what the Victorian Age thought was true about the nature of men and women and their relationships to each other. The French Lieutenant's Woman of the title, for example, is the dark, mysterious woman of the typical Victorian romantic novel. Sometimes the villainess, sometimes the heroine, such a woman was a symbol of what was forbidden. It is this aura of strangeness about Sarah Woodruff that first attracts Charles Smithson's attention. The story that develops around this pair echoes other romantic novels of a similar type, wherein a man falls in love with a strange and sometimes evil woman.

Charles' relationship with Ernestina Freeman creates another sort of romantic story, one that formed the basis of many Victorian novels. In the present story, the romantic situation which develops around the pair of aristocratic young people is not allowed to prevail over the forces, including the dark lady, that would normally keep Charles and Ernestina apart. Thus Fowles uses the popularity of the comedy of manners and combines it with the drama and sensationalism of the gothic novel and, using several stylistic conventions, creates a masterful, many-layered mystery that is one of the finest pieces of modern literature.

Critical Commentaries

Chapters 1-8

The initial chapter of the novel opens with an excerpt from Thomas Hardy's poem "The Riddle," which seems to describe the French Lieutenant's Woman as she is first seen by both the reader and by other characters in the story. She appears as an anonymous figure on the seashore, tragic and full of mystery. She is dressed in black and is staring intently at the sea; she appears to be the typical woman driven mad with grief by a lover who has left her.

In addition to the French Lieutenant's Woman, this chapter also introduces us to Ernestina Freeman, a lively, though somewhat conventional young woman. In a romantic novel, a girl such as Ernestina might play one of several roles. She could be the heroine, who proves to be more unconventional and adventuresome than she first appears. But if she is not destined to become the heroine herself, as is the case in this story, she becomes the bright and pretty rich girl who is a foil for the poor but intense young woman who is the actual heroine. This is the role which we suspect Ernestina will play in contrast to the dark intensity of the woman whose only name thus far is "Tragedy."

Charles Smithson is also quite traditional, though he would like to think that he isn't. He quotes Darwin and dabbles in paleontology. He represents the fashionable young man of his day, who rebels against what he sees as the stuffiness of his society, but who never rebels "too much."

The narrator, who is the persona of Fowles himself, is present at several points in the story. He both observes and manipulates his characters, as we shall see later in the novel. In keeping with the style of his tale, the narrator observes the couple and the lone figure on the beach. This device allows the author to introduce and describe his main characters, as well as allowing us a look at the setting where much of the action will take place. The chapter closes with a brief glimpse of the French Lieutenant's Woman herself.

Lyme Regis is a small English town set on a rocky shore. It was something of a resort or health retreat, as were many such villages at this time. The seaside was considered to be a healthy place to vacation because of its popular mineral springs. The larger cities were often smoke-filled, and people who could afford to travel were probably wise to go to smaller towns to breathe the fresh air.

Like many similar villages, Lyme Regis has not changed much in a hundred years, and even today one might find similar villages in some parts of the country, hardly changed except for the advent of electricity, automobiles, and television antennas. It is in just such a town that provincial attitudes might have lingered on, even at a time when many were experiencing change and upheaval in the cities. It is odd that Sarah, the French Lieutenant's Woman, chose Lyme Regis for her home, when she could have gone anywhere, for in Lyme Regis she would likely be designated as a fallen woman, whereas in London, she would have been fairly anonymous.

To introduce the second chapter, Fowles uses a quotation which states that there were at this time in England more women than men; this provides an implied commentary on the Victorian ideal of marriage as an appropriate goal for all women. If one assumes that the proper place of a woman is at a man's side, then some women will inevitably never reach that goal. Thus the character of the French Lieutenant's Woman must be defined in terms other than those defining her relationship to a man. Yet note how even her nickname, the "French Lieutenant's Woman," describes her in terms of her relationship with a, thus far, invisible man. The irony here is intentional.

This chapter delineates the interrelationships of the characters as they appear at the beginning of the story. The first focus is on the rather trite conversation between Charles and Ernestina. As they walk to the end of the Cobb, Charles sees the French Lieutenant's Woman, and Ernestina decides that she wants to turn back. In saying so, she gives Charles a brief account of the story of the "fallen woman," who, some say, is mad. Charles, who thinks of himself as a scientist, is more tolerant and more curious than Ernestina. Charles is both disturbed and fascinated by the mystery and romance that he perceives in the woman, though he will not admit that his curiosity goes beyond what he considers to be merely scientific.

Chapter 3 is largely a portrait of Charles, focusing on his relationship to his era. The author takes the opportunity to digress in a discussion of time. He compares the bustle of the twentieth century to the crawling pace of the previous century. Charles feels the ennui created by the slower pace of his century, though it should be noted that his boredom with life derives in part from the few demands which life makes upon him because of his favored social position. Charles is dissatisfied for reasons he cannot explain and, as a result, will prove to be easily attracted by that which is not only different or unusual, but which also has a hint of rarity about it. We see this already in his attraction to the mysterious woman, who represents that part of life not governed by the conventions he has unwillingly come to accept.

Charles is a rather typical romantic hero, a superficially cynical and a slightly tarnished yet inwardly idealistic Victorian gentleman. By Victorian standards he is somewhat jaded, but were he not so, he could not function as the typical romantic, rather Byronic hero. Love will rescue him. Charles' feelings about his sexuality are reminiscent of the struggles that the hero in Joyce's *Portrait of the Artist as a Young Man* undergoes when he is repulsed by his first sexual experiences. Charles' society has trained him to think that sex is evil, but then discourages him from giving it up. His father curses him when Charles desires to take Holy Orders; he sends him to Paris. There, Charles' youthful idealism finally gives way to a more cynical attitude that at least appears to accept the double standard that allows him his freedom, yet would ruin the reputation of a young woman not unlike "poor Tragedy."

The narrator then introduces us to two characters who are examples of the sort of hypocrisy that could, and sometimes did, flourish in Victorian society. Mrs. Poulteney calculates the arithmetical advantage of saving her soul by doing the not too inconvenient good deed of taking in a poor but refined gentlewoman. Mrs. Fairley, the housekeeper, is her "spy," who succeeds in making Sarah Woodruff's life miserable after she agrees to come and live with Mrs. Poulteney.

Both characters represent types that appear often in Victorian novels; they were the sort of person that the author's social criticism was frequently directed towards. Both Mrs. Poulteney and Mrs. Fairley are self-righteous and quite malicious. Although they profess to be good and moral Christians, they possess few Christian virtues. Instead, they believe themselves superior to someone such as Sarah, whose sins, real or imagined, have not warped her nature into a parody of morality.

Whether there were many real Victorian women who were as rigid and unthinking as this pair are is something to speculate about, but such characters were often present in the popular novels read by many women who probably had suffered at one time or another from the sharp tongues of their neighbors.

The quotation that prefaces Chapter 5 is from *In Memoriam,* which, according to the narrator, states that love can only be lust if there is no hope for immortality. In this chapter, which is largely a portrait of Ernestina, the narrator comments briefly on Victorian attitudes towards sexuality and duty, and the problems resulting therefrom.

Charles and Ernestina part, and Charles leaves for his hotel, while Ernestina returns to her room. There she contemplates herself in the mirror while undressing, until a stray thought of sex (about which she knows virtually nothing) occurs to her and, embarrassedly, she ceases admiring herself.

Not only are the descriptions and the dialogue couched in a style suitable for a Victorian novel, but even the narrator's interruptions, referring clearly to twentieth-century events, are also written in the formal English of a Victorian stylist such as George Eliot.

Returning to Mrs. Poulteney and the vicar, who is encouraging her to help Sarah Woodruff, we receive a more detailed description of Sarah and her encounter with the shipwrecked French lieutenant during the time when she was a governess for the children of Mr. and Mrs. Talbot of Charmouth.

Mrs. Poulteney decides to interview the girl in order to decide if she is a fitting object for the lady's dubious charity. She interprets Sarah's silence and habitual sad expression as an indication of feelings of remorse and takes her in. Although Sarah has earlier refused such charitable offers of employment from other people, she is destitute now and must accept the position. One of her reasons for accepting, which would have enraged Mrs. Poulteney had she suspected, was that Marlborough House possessed a good view of Lyme Bay, enabling Sarah to maintain her vigilant watch for the French Lieutenant who promised to return to her.

Fowles gives us a closer look in Chapter 7 at the relationships between the two main social classes that appear in the novel: the well-to-do middle class and their servants. The focus here is underscored by a quotation from one of the works of Karl Marx, in which he discusses the role of the servant class in an industrial society and its exploitation by the ruling classes.

As the chapter opens, it is the next morning and Charles is with his valet, Sam Farrow. Here, Sam is compared with Charles Dickens' character Sam Weller, a low-comedy servant whose image Sam Farrow tries to rise above. Whereas the servants of the 1830s seemed relatively content with their lot, the servants of the late 1860s began to sense and to demand a participation in the struggle referred to today as "upward mobility." The relationship between Charles and Sam is friendly, although to the reader Charles often appears patronizing in his condescending remarks to Sam. However, the narrator comments that this teasing relationship is probably preferable to the excessive formality of the *nouveau riche,* themselves the wealthy descendants of a working class.

In Chapter 8, Charles examines the seashore for fossils after having called on Ernestina and found that she would be indisposed until afternoon. He spends so much time there, however, that he has to take a shortcut back by an inland path. Inserted in this chapter is a discussion of Victorian attitudes towards scientific inquiry, and the public's lack of understanding of the significance of Darwin's discoveries. The scientific method, as we perceive it, was not widely used until quite recently by many who called themselves scientists. Many Victorians believed that all essential knowledge had already been discovered and what remained was to catalogue and arrange this body of knowledge.

Rather than propose hypotheses and attempt to prove or disprove them by using empirical methods of research and experimentation, many Victorians were very talented at arriving at ingenious theories to explain why certain phenomena existed. One example of this concerns the various theories offered to explain why fossils existed when the world was supposedly created in six days, approximately four thousand years before Christ was born. Such explanations were ingenious and often scholarly, but they were not scientific.

While Charles is considerably less hampered by some preconceived notions than his contemporaries, his idea of research in collecting fossils seems to be more of an excuse to avoid facing himself, who he is and who he wants to be. He plays the role of the gentleman, the dilettante naturalist, and then wonders why he is bored and dissatisfied with life. For Fowles, Charles' sort of scientific research, and that of this period in general, represents a sterile activity, where one examines minutae in order to avoid making major decisions and discoveries.

Chapters 9-17

In Chapter 9, we return to Sarah and Mrs. Poulteney, and Fowles presents an account of how Sarah manages to live with the dour old woman and is even able to attain some measure of freedom. In addition, Sarah intervenes on behalf of a maid, Millie, and wins herself the affection of Millie and the other servants. The popularity which Sarah gains among the servants brings with it the enmity of Mrs. Fairley, the housekeeper, who feels somewhat upstaged by Sarah.

Mrs. Fairley spies on Sarah and reports to Mrs. Poulteney what Sarah does and where she goes on her day off. Both women interpret Sarah's gazing at the sea as evidence that she has not fully repented of her infatuation with her seducer, the French Lieutenant. Mrs. Poulteney confronts Sarah with this matter of her unconvincing remorse. While Sarah manages to appear contrite, she says nothing, merely offering to leave. But rather than lose the companion whose services she has come to depend upon, Mrs. Poulteney agrees to a compromise. If Sarah will agree not to be seen too often on the seashore, Mrs. Poulteney will not forbid her to go there; thus, Sarah may go down to the sea at least occasionally. This appears to be a solution to the problem of Sarah's vaguely improper conduct. But at the close of the chapter Mrs. Fairley reports to her mistress that Sarah is now engaged in even more scandalous behavior: she has taken to walking on Ware Commons. We have yet to see why this is shocking, but we soon will, for Fowles clearly implies that young "ladies" do not stroll on Ware Commons, ever.

Charles, as we have seen, decided not long ago to take a shortcut home through some wild patches of seaside landscape called "Ware Commons" at its eastern end. This uninhabited and secluded patch of land was often used by couples as a meeting place, which resulted in its infamous reputation. Upon reaching a grassy meadow overlooking the ocean, Charles sees Sarah sleeping on a ledge below him. Entranced, he stares down at her until she suddenly awakes. He is embarrassed by his intrusion, apologizes, and leaves. But this chance encounter with the woman affects him deeply. He senses inituitively that she is innocent, no matter what she has done or not done. Without his being consciously aware of it, a part of him has forever rejected Victorian definitions of propriety and morality. We get a glimpse here of Victorian attitudes towards sex as revealed through Charles' concern about the woman whom society has made an outcast. He senses a disparity between what he is told is right and what he feels is right, a feeling that he cannot explain. But he knows that the cause of his discomfort is this strange woman.

Chapter 11 describes for us the meeting and subsequent engagement of Charles and Ernestina. As in many of Jane Austen's novels, the social and economic concerns that lay behind the marriage and courtship rituals of fashionable society are visible underneath all the romantic trimmings. Ernestina, deciding that she likes Charles much more than her other suitors, carefully plans how she will lure him into proposing, without seeming to be overly impressed by him at all. She succeeds. He proposes, thinking himself a fool for not having thought of it sooner.

Charles' own innocence and sexual inhibition are apparent in both this chapter and the preceding one. The author shows how Victorian ideas about such matters generally served to frustrate and confuse most people. We also see in Charles' encounters with Ernestina and with Sarah his awakening awareness of his own humanity and that of the opposite sex as well.

Charles stops at "the Dairy" on his way back to Lyme and purchases a bowl of cold milk. When Charles and the dairyman see Sarah walking back to town from Ware Commons, the man calls her "the French Loot'n'nt's Hoer," and Charles becomes angry but says nothing. He stops at Aunt Tranter's for tea with Ernestina and tells her of his hunting for fossils on Ware Commons. Although he is tempted to tell her about his meeting with Sarah, he senses that Ernestina would be disturbed, and thus carefully omits the tale of his spying on the sleeping woman. We again see Sarah and Ernestina juxtaposed and sense that both women are unconsciously acting in a manner determined for them, at least partly, by the social and economic dictates of their culture. Fowles' quotations from Marx and Tennyson at the beginning of this chapter tend to support this interpretation.

As Chapter 13 opens, Sarah is depressed after her encounter with Mrs. Poulteney, for Mrs. Poulteney has accused her of wanton behavior: she has been seen on Ware Commons, commonly believed to be a "lovers' lane." Sarah denies any such knowledge of the place and insists that she goes there simply to be alone, which is the truth. Sarah is exonerated, but just barely. We then see her at night, in her nightgown with her hair loose, staring out of her window. The narrator observes her, putting himself in the story again, as he will do at several points in the narrative. He tells us that although Sarah contemplates throwing herself from the window, she makes no move to do so.

This brings us to an important digression by the author. Fowles, the narrator, interrupts his story here to discuss the process of his writing, the autonomy of his characters, and his use of a pseudo-Victorian voice, in spite of the fact that his perspective derives strictly from the twentieth century. In this chapter he explicitly states his feelings about his style and methods that we have already perceived for ourselves in the narrative. It is for the reader to decide if such an explanation is necessary, but it might be noted that part of Fowles' purpose in writing this novel is to explore the genre of the novel and its possibilities, in addition to telling a story. Such commentary as Fowles inserts here serves to enable the reader to become aware of how this particular novel is part of a long tradition of novels in general and romantic novels in particular, and that he is as concerned with the form of his work as he is with its content.

In Chapter 14, Charles, Ernestina, and Aunt Tranter feel that they must pay obligatory visits to various members of Lyme society. The visit with Mrs. Poulteney is a bit of a fiasco, for she and Charles disagree about the proper methods of courtship. To Mrs. Poulteney, apparently, *no* methods are proper. She complains of Aunt Tranter's maid's relationship with Sam Farrow. Aunt Tranter believes that Mary is above reproach, but it is Charles who enters into an argument over it with Mrs. Poulteney. In the uncomfortable silence that follows the exchange, Charles and Sarah, who is also present, pass a quick glance of understanding. Sarah's discomfort and her feelings of awkwardness about being present at a social gathering where she feels out of place arouse Charles' sympathies. In addition, her empathy and Ernestina's apparent lack of it at this time cause Charles to become somewhat irritated with his fiancée. Meanwhile, Sam and Mary, the girl whose morals were discussed so freely, share a shy but sincere conversation in Aunt Tranter's kitchen. Their honesty is compared with the artificiality of the preceding conversation in Mrs. Poulteney's drawing room.

Several actual and potential relationships present themselves here, as Fowles examines the way various Victorians of different social classes view love. Sam and Mary, who have much less interest in the kind of respectability demanded by the upper classes, nevertheless base their courtship on a solid if simpler ground of what has been considered acceptable behavior for centuries. Yet even they are affected by trends in the standards of morality demanded by their society, though they are less conscious of rigidly observing them. Perhaps Charles suffers the most on this point, for he forms the half of a double standard who benefits by its hypocrisy, whether he wishes to or not. His awareness that he is allowed to do things that no woman would be permitted to do does bother him, though he rarely reaches the point where he can question it, beyond his mild efforts here in Mrs. Poulteney's parlour.

One cannot discuss Victorian concepts of morality or appropriate behavior without noting the position of Sarah, the outcast, the fallen woman. Because of her self-admitted status, she is forever excluded from polite society. Yet we shall later see that changes in Sarah's life and in late Victorian society in general render the role she has chosen for herself obsolete.

Later, at home, Charles unkindly teases Sam about the way that he treats the local girls, but Sam asserts his sincerity—he truly loves Mary. Observing Charles and Sam together again, we notice how differently Charles acts in various social contexts, using different voices, so to speak, depending upon whether he is talking to Sam, to Sarah, to Ernestina, or to Mrs. Poulteney. Charles later becomes vaguely aware of this duplicity, but he is at a loss to understand it fully, for it is an activity in which we all participate.

In Chapter 16, we encounter some of the more domestic aspects of Charles and Ernestina's courtship. Ernestina acts as the dutiful wife-to-be, and Charles is somewhat disturbed by her meekness, perhaps because at the edge of his conscious awareness is the realization that this demure person is not the real Ernestina Freeman.

Here Fowles adds an aside on the lives and status of Victorians: there were often rebels, gentle or otherwise, but, alas, he implies Ernestina is not one of them. She is singularly ignorant of any deficiencies in the status of women in her time. By comparing the lives of Ernestina and Sarah, one could infer that part of the reason Sarah is able to see some of the injustice women experience in Victorian society is that her education and economic position are so disparate. Ernestina, by comparison, is relatively secure in her position in society, and thus is less inclined to question it. In addition, Charles accepts the way things are, for he could not imagine any other sort of society existing, but his wider experience causes him to notice anomalies and to experience discomfort because of them, without understanding why. Charles' awareness of the ambiguity created by the mores of his culture makes it possible for him to become Sarah's confidant. A different man would have seen her as a different sort of woman.

The chapter ends with another encounter between Charles and Sarah on the cliffs above the sea. While climbing the rocks in search of fossils, Charles again meets Sarah. He is struck by the intense sensuality that she radiates, but he will hardly admit this to himself. Instead, they discuss, with some awkwardness and embarrassment, Sarah's history. Then suddenly, Sarah makes a startling confession: her French Lieutenant is married; more important, she is not waiting for him. Charles is stunned by this revelation, for it makes the motivation of her odd behavior more difficult to fathom than it was before. Charles does not yet realize it, but he is becoming more and more attracted to this strange young woman.

Later, Charles, Aunt Tranter, and Ernestina attend a concert, and although it is a Lenten concert of sacred music, even this is frowned upon by some members of the community as being too frivolous. Ernestina gaily chatters and makes comments about the people they see, and Charles is slightly irritated with her youthful flippancy. Her liveliness seems shallow to him compared with the serious intensity of Sarah. But then he feels guilty for even entertaining such unkind thoughts, and he proceeds to brood about his condition. He has a vague feeling of being trapped by the tedious conventionality of polite society without knowing why he feels so. Yet he is at the same time somewhat happily resigned to soon having Ernestina as his wife.

We next see a brief scene between Sam and Mary. We are shown how completely Sam has fallen in love with Mary's innocence and her solidity. She would be a good and kind wife who would fit, he believes, into the future he plans for himself as an independent tradesman.

The complexity of Charles' feelings about Ernestina are juxtaposed with the simplicity of Sam's feelings for Mary. Sam and Mary's courtship is truly romantic, while Charles and Ernestina's is much more the result of a variety of social, economic, and personal influences that affect both his and her decision to marry one another. Thus, the closing line of this chapter is ironic in the context of the subject of this romantic novel. Sam and Mary are incidental characters, yet they are lovers in the truest sense.

Chapters 18-21

Charles again meets Sarah by the seashore, quite unintentionally, of course, but by now his walks to the shore are colored by his fears and also his hopes of meeting her. She gives him two fossils she has found, then tentatively turns to him for his help. She wants him to hear her full story. He misunderstands and, consequently, offers other sorts of aid; for example, he suggests that she talk to the sympathetic Aunt Tranter. But it is not mere kindness that Sarah wants. She seems to want Charles to understand her and her situation, matters that he is hardly capable of perceiving at this point, for he thinks in terms of one's conduct and its impact on the individual's relationship to society. Hence, he advises her to leave Lyme and begin life anew somewhere where she isn't known. She refuses. She does not want to hide from herself, though the totality of what she does want is by no means clear. After much discussion, Charles reluctantly agrees to meet Sarah again and to allow her to tell him about herself.

It is safe to say that Sarah does not yet realize that she is attracted to Charles in ways that go beyond the mere perception that he is more sensitive than most people whom she has met. Charles is likewise attracted to Sarah, but he struggles against what he feels would be a dangerous relationship. His conventional background deludes him into thinking that he has agreed to be Sarah's confessor from the highest of motives only. It is true that he does want to help her, but he carries deep within himself the sniggering suspicion that his motives for wanting to see her aren't entirely selfless.

Charles, Ernestina, and Aunt Tranter share a meal that evening with Dr. Grogan, a hearty Irish physician. The uninhibited conversation of Dr. Grogan and Aunt Tranter disturbs Ernestina a bit, for she is the product of a later and more rigid upbringing than they were. Charles and Dr. Grogan return later to the doctor's rooms for a drink and discuss science, Darwin, and Sarah Woodruff. They attempt to bring their knowledge of science to the problem they feel she presents. The doctor believes that she suffers from a vague disorder labeled "melancholia" because she fails to take any action, such as leaving town, that might relieve her suffering. He rightly perceives that Mrs. Poulteney's home is probably the worst possible place she could have chosen to live, and he agrees with Charles that the only solution to Sarah's problem is that she must leave Lyme. This conversation with the doctor enables Charles to soothe his guilty feelings about allowing Sarah to confide in him, for he can feel that he, as an objective but sympathetic listener, can help her where others have failed.

Charles and Dr. Grogan believe that they, as enlightened rationalists, can understand and solve Sarah's problems. They believe she is seriously disturbed, possibly on the verge of madness. Their reasoning is ironic, considering the purported rigorousness of the moral standards of the time. They believe that Sarah's irrationality is related to her feelings of alienation from normal society because she was once seduced. They discuss how similar things have happened to many other women, yet these women have gone on to marry and live normal lives.

We next encounter Sarah and Millie. Following her illness, Millie has taken a room next to Sarah's. The young maid is afraid of the dark and often sleeps with Sarah for comfort; there, the arms of the older girl give her the sole sense of security she has known in her short, difficult life. The meeting between Sarah and Millie illustrates the contrast between the almost wordless rapport of the girls and the highly abstract and rationalized behavior of the two men. The narrator inserts modern explanations of Darwinism, social reform, and lesbianism, all of which, as Fowles intends, fail to explain the events as the reader perceives them. Dr. Grogan and Charles do not understand Sarah, nor would a modern psychologist be accurately explaining Sarah's relationship to Millie by referring to it as lesbianism. The point of these digressions by Fowles is that there is no one answer to Sarah's problems. Answers only partially explain the complex fictional world that Fowles has created. He implies that the problems posed by the situations which the characters find themselves in do not lend themselves to simple solutions.

Charles and Sarah meet again in Chapter 20 as they agreed to do, and Sarah reveals the story of herself and the French Lieutenant. His ship was wrecked not far from shore, and all but two of the crew were drowned. Captain Talbot brought the survivors ashore, and Lieutenant Varguennes, whose leg was seriously injured, was nursed in the captain's home. Sarah, who was the governess for the Talbot children, helped to nurse him. However, as he recovered he began to take an interest in Sarah, and he teased and flirted with her. Sarah's knowledge of French was limited, and Varguennes spoke little English. As a result, their playful banter had an air of unreality for Sarah, and she was easily beguiled by the charming Lieutenant. After his recovery was complete, the Lieutenant traveled to a neighboring town to board a ship for home. He told Sarah to meet him there so they could say their farewells. Sarah states that she did follow him, but found him staying at a disreputable hotel. At that point she realized how shallow he really was, and she also realized the true nature of his affection for her. But then, in an odd combination of defiance and despair, she gave herself to him, knowing that she would never see him again, and knowing that she did not want to see him, ever.

The willfulness of Sarah's act is inexplicable to Charles. Her explanation, however, is simple. She tells Charles that she did not give herself to Varguennes as an act of love, or even of sensuality. Her decision was made on the basis of what we might today call a political act of defiance. She would be changed; society would be forced to acknowledge her existence. Yet this explanation only further mystifies Charles. Had Sarah been seduced or raped, or had she even thought herself to be in love, Charles would have understood, but the abstract determination, the sense of committing herself to a chosen destiny that lies beyond her act, is unfathomable to him. The mystery surrounding her is increased by the apparent unreason of her choice of a lover. Charles is both shocked and stimulated by her confession. She has only added to her aura of romance and mystery. For Charles, she is even more of an idealized dark romantic figure, a woman who is attractive and compelling because she is such an enigma.

At this point one should keep the question in mind as to what Sarah's true motives are. Was her impetuous act really more of an act of defiance against the limits her society had placed upon her, or was it the result of the confusion and despair of a young girl? What lies behind her desire to tell all these things about herself to Charles Smithson, a man she barely knows?

Sarah continues her confession, attempting to explain how little the fact that Varguennes was married really mattered to her. She discovered that he was married about a month after he left, and even by then it did not matter. Already she was playing the role of martyr and pariah, for she had made no secret of her rendezvous with the Lieutenant.

Charles points out that it is absurd for her to condemn herself so thoroughly. He uses Dr. Grogan's argument that many women have suffered worse and, at least, appear to live normal lives in spite of their experiences. Sarah counters his argument, stating that such women perceive themselves as outcasts, but lack the courage to admit that they have acted contrary to the rules of society. They become secret pariahs, while Sarah is a visible one. The two then talk further, and Charles becomes uncomfortably aware of his attraction for her. But he tells himself that perhaps he has been able to convince her to save herself.

Suddenly, they hear a noise and, looking around, they see Sam and Mary. Charles is afraid of being caught with Sarah, but the other young people do not see them. Sam and Mary move away, and Charles and Sarah separate, presumably for the last time. Charles goes back to town, rather guiltily congratulating himself on his narrow escape; he believes that his sincere desire to help Sarah has succeeded. The excuse that his interest in her is purely charitable enables him to justify to himself his otherwise suspiciously clandestine meetings with Sarah.

Charles is, of course, deluding himself, as is Sarah. Although she is not fully aware of it, she is disappointed that he has not expressed or acted upon his attraction for her. Instead, he has insisted on acting in a manner that, to her, is false. She is disappointed too by his conventionality: he is too thoroughly the Victorian gentleman. But at the same time, she doesn't realize what such disappointment implies; she does not fully understand that her reasons for wanting to see him are as mixed as his are.

Charles is still savoring his relief at escaping from the snare of Sarah's attractiveness as he returns to town and finds a telegram waiting for him at his hotel. His uncle at Winsyatt asks that he make an immediate visit to discuss some important matters. Charles is overjoyed for two reasons: first, the message provides a perfect excuse to leave Lyme for awhile, thus saving him from having to explain his activities, should he be asked to do so. Second, he believes that the subject of the discussion will be concerned with his upcoming marriage, and that his uncle wishes to know which of the two houses the young couple will settle in once they are wed.

The sumptuous estate in which Charles' uncle lives is given a lengthy description: we read about the lands, the people, and of Charles' fond memories of them. He is especially charmed at again seeing Mrs. Hawkins, the laundrymaid, for she was a substitute mother for the mother-less boy. The elaborate treatment given this description of the estate enables the author to comment on the lot of the people who worked on such estates as compared to that of the downtrodden poor of London and other industrial cities. The life of these country people was considerably more pleasant than that of their urban counterparts. Although they were poor, they worked in pleasant surroundings and were often treated quite well by the gentry.

However, our admiration for the country life is cut short when we discover, along with Charles, the reason he has been asked to visit. Instead of seeing his uncle, Charles is greeted by an empty house that has been mysteriously redecorated. Even the bustard, a grouse-like bird which Charles had shot long ago, and which his uncle had cherished and had had stuffed, was missing.

The scene now focuses upon Charles' return to Aunt Tranter's house, and we learn what passed between him and his uncle. As the reader might have guessed, Charles' uncle has decided to marry a young widow, Mrs. Tomkins. Ernestina is enraged on Charles' behalf, or so she says, but Charles is a bit embarrassed by the vehemence of her protests at the unfairness of his uncle's decision. Changing the subject, Charles asks what news has occurred in Lyme, and he is told that Mrs. Poulteney has dismissed Sarah Woodruff, and that she has since disappeared. Charles is stunned. He leaves abruptly, wondering how much of his association with Sarah is known and whether she was dismissed because she was seen with him on Ware Commons. He goes immediately to the White Lion, the inn where Sarah's things were sent.

The White Lion, coincidentally, is also where Charles is staying. Back in his rooms there, his extreme agitation becomes evident. He finds two notes that Sarah has left for him: a sealed one written in English, urgently requesting that he see her one more time, and an unsealed note in French, telling Charles where he can find her. Charles attempts to discover who sent the notes, which arouses Sam's suspicion. He hastily orders Sam to attend to dinner, but then leaves in a hurry without eating anything.

Chapter 26 continues to focus on the effects of Charles' sudden change of fortune. While Sam sits in Charles' sitting room, he contemplates how he can manipulate his employer to his own advantage, for Sam suspects that Charles is more deeply involved with the strange woman, Sarah Woodruff, than he would care to have anyone discover. Sam's ultimate loyalty, however, is to himself and his future wife, Mary. Now that Charles cannot hope with any confidence to receive the inheritance which his uncle had promised him, Sam Farrow must plan his future carefully.

At this point, Fowles provides us with Sam's memories of his and Charles' visit to Winsyatt and Charles' discovery that the heir to his uncle's fortune will be the child of Mrs. Tomkins.

As Charles' financial status has changed, so do his feelings about his relationships with the people around him. He is still cautious regarding his involvement with Sarah, but he is less apt to deny that he is involved with her, at least to himself. We also can see that the attitudes of others towards Charles are also altered.

Disturbed about Sarah, and doubtful about his commitment to Ernestina, Charles goes to see his friend Doctor Grogan again. The doctor suggests that Charles leave Lyme for awhile, and he will attempt to help Sarah if he can. He views Charles' infatuation with the woman as an aberration that could threaten the young man's marriage to Ernestina. He advises Charles to confess to his fiancée that he has seen Sarah, and says further that Sarah's actions appear to be those of a woman who might be mad, and the doctor is convinced that she might have to be incarcerated in an insane asylum. This shocks Charles, for he does not believe that Sarah is motivated by madness, though he does find her behavior strange.

In an effort to show Charles the true nature of Sarah Woodruff, the doctor gives Charles a book that describes the court trial of another French lieutenant: Lieutenant Emile de La Roncière, who in 1835 was apparently framed by a woman not unlike Sarah, in the doctor's opinion. On very slight evidence, the man was convicted of sexually assaulting the woman and served a prison sentence.

This conflict between Charles' love for Ernestina and for Sarah will encompass a major portion of the novel, but the resolution of the conflict will not complete the story, as we shall see. In addition to emphasizing how disturbed Charles is over Sarah, Chapter 27 illustrates still another interpretation of Sarah's actions—that is, Dr. Grogan sees in her puzzling behavior the symptoms of mental illness, as defined by the psychological knowledge of the era. The reader can see here the assumptions held by many people of this time about the nature of the human psyche. A woman who did not fit the established criteria of a contented female member of society—passive, modest, weak, and unsensual—was likely to be labeled insane. There was a close connection between a woman's sexual behavior, or lack of it, and her role in society. It was, in short, believed by many people at this time that a proper woman didn't enjoy sex; if she did, there was something wrong with her.

Chapters 28-32

Here, Fowles inserts a recounting of Lieutenant de La Roncière, based on the evidence of Marie de Morell, the sixteen-year-old daughter of Roncière's commanding officer. Marie, it seems, provided false evidence in the form of "poison-pen threats" allegedly written by Roncière. Although numerous contemporary observers of the trial protested the verdict, Roncière was found guilty and sentenced to ten years imprisonment. Later discussions of the case note the personality disturbances of young Marie, and present evidence indicates that Roncière was innocent of her accusations.

Dr. Grogan gives this information to Charles, hoping he will find some similarities between the story of this woman and her French lieutenant, and the situation Sarah appears to find herself in. The doctor quite honestly believes that Sarah is emotionally unbalanced and suffers from the same melancholia that was thought to plague many young women. His diagnosis indicates an interesting example of the Victorian attitude towards women. While women were often idealized as being pure, loving, kind, and nurturing, they were also seen as being weak, childlike, and subject to all manner of illnesses. Often a woman's perfectly normal expressions of strong will or emotion were taken to indicate that she was unbalanced or even insane.

The author of the article about Lieutenant de La Roncière discusses ways in which hysterical young women attempted to attract attention to themselves. However, in a footnote, Fowles indicates that although this particular Victorian physician was zealous in placing all the blame on Marie, Roncière did in fact have some part in the case, though not nearly the role Marie implied. Thus he casts a doubt that even the enlightened discoveries of psychology and medicine can claim to answer human problems or fully describe human situations.

Charles finishes reading the account, but remains unconvinced. His memory of Sarah does not resemble the portrait which he has just examined of Marie de Morell. He changes his clothes and decides that he will go to see Sarah himself. He is apprehensive about Grogan's judgment of Sarah and does not wish to see her incarcerated. He also cannot resist the temptation to see her again. He is singularly unaware of his true motives, knowing little about what he really desires. What is interesting, as we shall see, is that Sarah does not fathom her own motives, in spite of the apparent singleness of her vision.

Thus, early in the morning, Charles goes to the derelict cottage used by the man from the dairy for storing hay, the building that Sarah described in her note. The place appears deserted, but Charles looks over a stall, half-fearing to find her dead and sees her, sleeping.

Chapter 30 is a flashback to Sarah's earlier confrontation with Mrs. Poulteney, which led to her dismissal and sudden disappearance. Mrs. Poulteney, as usual, is self-rightous and vindictive. She gives Sarah an envelope and tells her to leave. Sarah asks to know why she is being dismissed, although she is aware that Mrs. Fairly saw her on Ware Commons, possibly with Charles although it is unlikely that he was seen. Mrs. Poulteney calls Sarah a "public scandal," an accusation about which Sarah says absolutely nothing except that she will leave. She even refuses her wages, suggesting that Mrs. Poulteney take the money to buy an instrument of torture to use on those who are unfortunate enough to come into association with her. This retort upsets Mrs. Poulteney so thoroughly that she dramatically falls into a faint. Sarah then goes to her room and cries herself to sleep. She decides that she will leave the next morning.

Fowles returns his narrative to Charles. Looking over the partition, our hero sees Sarah asleep. His desire to protect her overwhelms him and, as he talks to her, he tries to convince her to leave Lyme. Then the real reason that he has sought her out yet one more time overtakes him, and they embrace. This scene occurs several times in the book; Charles, at one point, agrees to meet Sarah one more time, only to succumb to feelings of passionate physical attraction rather than the altruistic "duty" he thinks he is feeling.

Back at Aunt Tranter's house, Ernestina is tense, with good cause; she is disturbed about her minor argument with Charles, but has vowed in her diary to be more loving and dutiful, a note that strikes falsely with her normally wry attitude. Fowles explains that she is a victim of her environment and her upbringing. In spite of a valuable sense of irony, she is still a proper young lady and she tries to conform.

We also discover that Sam has decided to leave Charles, which upsets Mary considerably. But we should realize by now that Sam is exploitative in his relationship with Charles and that he feels justified in getting what he can from him.

Chapters 33-37

Returning to the hay-shed where Charles and Sarah are discovered by Sam and Mary, we witness Charles and Sam confronting one another. Sam now knows for certain, though he had suspected before, that Charles is involved with Sarah. Sam's desire that Charles marry Ernestina is threatened by this relationship, but he hopes at this point that his tacit agreement with Charles to be silent about Sarah will place him in a position to influence Charles. Sam realizes that he may have to blackmail Charles to prod him to marry Ernestina, but as of yet, he has made no definite plans. Charles, by contrast, naively assumes that Sam is absolutely loyal. There is much irony in the two men's perception of each other.

Sam and Mary leave, and Charles warns Sarah that Dr. Grogan has mentioned committing her to any asylum. Both are appalled at this idea, and Sarah is convinced she must leave. She plans to go to Exeter.

Later, Charles talks to Ernestina and tries to explain that he must leave for a time. She is upset, but not surprised, for she has suspected that he has been having a relationship with Sarah. The exchange is stiff and false, and Charles also meets Mary, a witness of the morning's events, but she, too, will say nothing, so long as her beloved Sam tells her not to.

Just at the time that Charles and Ernestina's relationship becomes more and more of a charade, and Charles hides his true feelings and Ernestina hides her fears and suspicions, Sam and Mary grow even more strongly devoted to each other. Sam will stop at nothing to gain some measure of security for himself and his future wife, and he is a prototype of the ambitious and struggling young businessman who will dominate much of the twentieth century. There are more similarities between Sam and Ernestina's father, Mr. Freeman, than the latter would guess, or care to admit if he did consider them.

Chapter 35 consists of a long digression discussing the role of women in relation to Victorian ideas of sexuality. From this general discussion we return to the courtship of Sam and Mary, one that follows the customs of their period and their class.

One might note that most of the ideas about women's sexuality or lack of it were generated by and for the middle classes. The great number of rural and working classes paid a minimum amount of attention to such repressive notions and lived and married much as they always did. Many of the Victorian conceptions of sexuality dealt with their ideals of the romantic marriage, an ideal which often contradicted the economic realities of marriage and courtship.

Women were treated as "special creatures," things to be admired and cherished. But this admiration carried with it a view that women were helpless and childlike, which, for the majority, resulted in a narrow and restricted life. They may have been cherished and pampered, but women of the middle classes were often just plain bored. Even continuous childbearing didn't serve to keep them occupied, since their servants contributed most of the work involved in caring for children. For the poor, the ideals of Victoria made little change in their lives; they worked long and hard and received no emotional or financial remuneration.

After Sarah goes to Exeter, she takes up residence at Endicott's Family Hotel, a rather disreputable place in the poorer section of town. With a portion of the money which Charles has given her to live on, she buys a few things—a dark green merino shawl and a Toby jug. She is excited that she is actually purchasing and owning something. Finally she has done what has always been denied her. We see the contrast of her natural dignity and simplicity against the utter poverty of her surroundings.

One might compare the apparent serenity of Sarah's quiet life at the hotel with the quotation from Tennyson's *In Memoriam* in which he alludes to the passion underlying many of Sarah's seemingly innocent acts. This suggests that there is more going on in Sarah's mind at this moment than is apparent in this chapter.

The last sentence in the chapter, "Then she began to eat, and without any delicacy whatsoever," brings us back to the implication that Sarah is a more earthy and passionate creature than either she appears at this moment, or than her society would have us believe of women in general.

Sarah, unlike Ernestina, does not *have* to be a lady, which in Victorian terms, meant denying that she had a body, or was capable of feeling passion or desire. Women were, as we have noted, believed to be delicate creatures: if they thought too much or studied too hard or exerted themselves physically, they became ill. Many people even believed that a lady was not capable of enjoying sexual intercourse with her husband. There was a joke to that effect, in which the husband advised his wife on performing her wifely duty. "Just lie back, Dear, and think of England." However, if a woman was poor, she must have been much healthier, from society's point of view, for the poor (men, women, and children) worked long hours doing difficult jobs in factories and mines, and only the hardy survived.

The feminist movement was beginning in England at this time, along with other reform movements. Although women were barely beginning to question their circumscribed lives, some slow progress was being made towards a measure of social and economic freedom.

Returning to Charles' problems, we listen as he meets with Mr. Freeman to inform him of his changed prospects. While the latter is somewhat surprised at what he hears, this change does not alter Charles' marrying Ernestina, in Mr. Freeman's opinion. In addition, the two discuss a topic that they previously were reluctant to discuss—that is, the possibility of Charles' future employment in Mr. Freeman's company. Charles, Mr. Freeman says, would be an executive of course, and we should be aware that in this period there was a sharp distinction drawn between those who worked in trade for a living, even when they owned the company, and those who inherited their wealth.

The interview is eventually concluded, evidently to the satisfaction of both parties, and Charles is led in to meet Mrs. Freeman. We see his discomfort with these people, which stems partly from his backgound of old wealth and from his doubts, still largely unadmitted, about his marriage to Ernestina. Charles later admits that he hoped Mr. Freeman would cancel the wedding when he told the gentleman of the probable loss of both his inheritance and his title. He is, of course, feeling disappointed and trapped. Mr. Freeman still approves of the marriage. Charles also feels guilty because he should feel grateful for Mr. Freeman's generous offers of employment and future help for the couple, but he does not.

Chapters 38-44

Charles leaves the Freeman residence in London. The foggy evening outside provides an apt metaphor for his depressed mood. He does not know why he attempted to impress upon his future father-in-law the gravity of his reduced circumstances, but it is apparent to the reader that Charles vaguely hoped that Ernestina's parents would not allow her to marry him.

For this reason, he is looking to external events to help him resolve the conflict between his attraction to Sarah and his duty to Ernestina.

He walks through London and, while doing so, he inadvertently passes by Mr. Freeman's large shop. The thought of actually working there gives him a feeling of nausea. He sincerely believes that his repugnance is based on his conviction as a scholar and as a scientist that life should mean more than merely acquiring money. But actually some of his animosity towards working in trade is based on his upbringing as a member of the upper classes; he can't help but feel that working is somehow beneath him and, he fears that he will lose his self-respect if he eventually accepts Mr. Freeman's values. He is in despair about his fate. He hails a cab in order to seek refuge at an institution that persists even today: his club.

The tone of this chapter indicates that although Charles' marriage to Ernestina is still a definite prospect, he is dismayed rather than reassured by this. There is a great deal of irony in Fowles' handling of Charles' attitudes towards his dilemma. He is influenced and inhibited by what is considered proper behavior for a Victorian gentleman, just as his fiancée is governed by what is considered proper for a lady.

Charles goes to his club and he meets two fellow members whom he has known from his college days. These two aristocrats are stereotypes of Victorian decadent young rakes. Together they drink milk punch, followed by champagne, and soon persuade the now inebriated Charles to accompany them in pursuit of an evening's pleasure. The three men go to a brothel where they witness an exotic dance, after which the dancers join them. Charles, however, revolted by these surroundings and activities, leaves. As he rides off alone, he finds himself propositioning a young woman who reminds him of Sarah.

In this chapter, Charles' behavior reflects his confused and anguished state of mind. We might also note, however, his discomfort with what was, to many people of this time (and the present), an acceptable pastime. He vaguely senses that not all the women in the brothel enjoy their work and that they may be victims of exploitation. Fowles perhaps perceives this paradox of the role of the prostitute in Victorian society; this is suggested by the quotation he chooses to open the chapter with, taken from a letter supposedly written by a prostitute, protesting the way society shuns and scorns her and yet seeks her services. Although Sarah is not a prostitute, this letter shows how similar the problems of these professional fallen women are to Sarah's in a society that both scorns and exploits their supposed immorality.

Charles and the girl go to her rooms, and he is touched by what he

feels is her innocence in spite of her profession, particularly by the sol-
icitude she shows towards her sleeping child in the next room. However,
whatever his intentions are, Charles never succeeds in completing what he
begins. He asks her name, and when she casually replies that her name is
Sarah, the shock and his own drunken state combine to make him physically ill. But Charles' nausea is more than physical. He believes that he is
forever deprived of that mystery in his life that would both save him and
free him, namely Sarah Woodruff. Whether or not the author really intends
Sarah to be Charles' savior, however, remains to be seen.

The next morning Charles is horribly hung over, but he recalls all too
clearly the events of the night before and remembers how the girl Sarah
calmly held his head while he was sick, and then went and got a cab for
him. While she was out, Charles comforted her baby, who had started
crying. When she returned he left a rather large amount of money for her.
As he got into the cab, he saw her run after him and thank him for the
money.

Although Charles feels wretched, he begins to take what appears to be
a more realistic look at his present situation. He feels that his rakish
evening was perhaps simply a gesture of farewell to the single life and that
he will now settle down to marriage with Ernestina and a job with her
father's company. Sam informs him that he plans to ask Mary to marry
him, hoping that Charles will advance the young couple 250 pounds towards setting up their own haberdashery. Sam realizes that his future now
may depend on the dowry that Ernestina will bring, since Charles no longer
can expect an inheritance from his uncle. Thus Sam is especially interested
in what Charles does, and feels increasingly threatened by the possibility
that Charles won't marry Ernestina.

Sarah has left a note at Charles' hotel, containing only the address of
her hotel in Exeter. He resolves to ignore the implied invitation and prepares to return to Lyme. He has decided to go ahead with his plans to marry
Ernestina and feels somewhat reconciled to his fate. He and Sam take a
carriage back the way they came. They stop in Exeter, where Charles
knows that Sarah Woodruff is staying, but Charles says that they will
continue their journey rather than stop for the night. This is the beginning
of the section of the novel in which Fowles presents us with several possible endings for Charles, Ernestina, and Sarah. Here, we are shown Charles
and the possible outcome of the story if his embryonic romance with Sarah
were to be terminated at this point.

Charles and Sam arrive in Lyme, and Charles goes to see Ernestina.
Their banter is concluded with his retelling of a trivialized version of his

encounter with Sarah. Fowles then enters to tell us briefly how Charles and Ernestina, Sam and Mary, and other characters we have met, lived their lives, begat families, and died, if not with great joy, certainly without great sadness. He also, in the course of this digression, discusses the fate of Mrs. Poulteney when she finally goes to meet her celestial reward. He creates a fantasy about the soul of Mrs. Poulteney, who has recently died, and how it fares in heaven. She arrives at the pearly gates and expects to be treated with the deference she received when she was alive. However, much to her surprise and the gratification of the reader, she is summarily turned away. Thus, the whimsical and playful tone of the last half of the chapter prepares us for the revelation that the first half, the reunion of Charles and Ernestina, is also merely an imaginative aside, a speculation on what might have happened if Charles had returned to Lyme when he was supposed to, which he didn't.

Chapters 45 and 46

At last, we realize the "truth" about the events of the novel: at Exeter, Charles decided to stop for the night, not consciously realizing it, but intending all the same to visit Sarah. He still believes that his visit is nothing more than an attempt to end the affair in a fashionably Victorian way.

Charles finds Sarah's hotel and goes to her room, where she is resting an injured foot. They speak of minor things and Charles is overcome by the realization that he came, not to say goodbye, but simply because he felt compelled to see her again. They embrace and, finally acknowledging their passion, he carries her to bed.

Fowles notes at the end of the chapter that this passionate scene occurred in only ninety seconds. The implication is that Fowles takes a rather ironic attitude towards the concept of the romantic novel, since all that "love" seems to amount to is a few words and a brief coupling. Even the most passionate moments, he seems to say, are only a small portion of existence. This ironic tone will occur again, especially in scenes that are supposedly typical of romantic novels.

Chapter 47

The two lovers lie in each other's arms. We see this moment from Charles' point of view. His conduct horrifies him, as it can only horrify a Victorian gentleman who believes that no well-bred woman enjoys or desires physical lovemaking. Furthermore, we see an interesting contrast in this chapter when he idealizes Sarah. She is perfect, an angel, and he can think of no other course of action than to marry her. But she gently tells him that she is unworthy of him, though she never explains why. It is enough, she insists, that she knows he loves her, and that under other circumstances they might have married. He doesn't argue any more, but says that he will think about what to do for a few days.

As he gets up and proceeds to get dressed in the next room, he discovers blood on himself. At first he thinks he has injured himself, but then realizes that she was a virgin. He suddenly understands fully that everything she said and did was based on a lie. She had never given herself to Varguennes. It is here that we see the other side of Charles' concept of her. Now, instead of seeing her as an angel, Charles can only believe that she is a temptress, a demon, and a wicked woman who for some unknown reason, perhaps blackmail, wanted to seduce him. Yet he is still perplexed by what she has done, and he wants to know why. Sadly, she says she does not know. She does love him, but insists that they cannot marry. Sarah asks him to leave, addressing him as Mr. Smithson. He is hurt by her return to formality. She has told him that he has given her something to live for, the knowledge that he might have loved her. But he cannot comprehend what little explanation she is able to give. She orders him to leave and finally he does.

The two images that Charles has of Sarah are illustrated here. We cannot conceive of her except in terms of some romantic ideal. She is a woman of mystery, an angel, and finally a woman of mystery again, but this time one who, to him, has sinister overtones.

The impression that the reader gets from this chapter is that Sarah is none of the women Charles thinks she is; she is simply a human being. This does not fully explain why she acted the way she did in her relationship with Charles, but although we do not know the secrets of her motives, we know that Charles' conclusions are wrong. It is worthwhile to remember that Sarah, for reasons of her own, was playing the role of the fallen woman long before Charles arrived in Lyme. Yet something apparently happened to her when she met Charles, just as he was affected when he met her. They were attracted to each other and, without really understanding why, they fell in love. Had these events occurred under other circumstances their relationship might have evolved along other lines. But that is another story.

Chapters 48-55

Charles, distraught by his encounter with Sarah, confronts himself. He leaves Endicott's Family Hotel, walking rapidly down a street in a poorer section of Exeter. He passes a church and is drawn to it. As he enters, the curate tells Charles that it is closing time. Charles asks if he might stop and pray a moment. The curate, seeing that Charles is a gentleman, gives him the keys to the church and asks him to lock it when he leaves. Charles kneels and mumbles a prayer to himself, but the image of Sarah keeps rising before him. In despair he weeps, not only over what he has done, or lost with Sarah, but also over the fact that there is no comfort or forgiveness to be found in religion as he understands it.

The Victorians were still adhering to the old, structured ways of believing in God, but were continually torn by changes in their society that threatened that structure. They wanted to believe, but feared that they did not. Faced with this dilemma, common to many of his time, Charles makes an intuitive leap. He feels that he understands the message of Christ conveyed by the crucifix in the church in a new way. It is not the dying figure on the cross that is significant, but rather the example of the living Christ who wanted people to live rightly, to be kind, and to be good that was the true meaning of religion. His inspiration is followed by a dialogue with himself in which he comes to terms with his actions. Although for the first time he sees what his true feelings for Sarah are, he has come to no decision regarding what to do about her or about Ernestina. All he knows is that he wishes to do the right thing, which at this point appears to be honestly facing how he really feels. Although he has made no decision as of yet, he intuitively feels that he cannot marry Ernestina if he does not really love her. He has not yet expressed this thought except in the vaguest way, but it supports his actions and his thoughts regarding his fiancée.

Charles returns the key to the curate after leaving the church, concluding as he does so, that he is finished with institutionalized religion. However, this does not undermine the truth of his feelings that he experienced when he was in the church, but rather emphasizes the gap between inner perception and outward, socially acceptable forms that a few people of his time were beginning to perceive.

Fowles develops this duality further, discussing the difficulty that Victorians had in reconciling the disparate impulses of the body and soul. Charles illustrates this duality in his belief that he cannot freely express his love for Sarah until he has freed himself of his obligation to Ernestina. Unlike others of his time, Charles does not ignore his essential feelings about Sarah, and his lack of a similar feeling for Ernestina. Though he may have attempted to do so too late, he tries to follow an inner guide rather than allow the conventions of proper society to govern his acts. He chooses a perilous course of action.

After returning to the hotel, Charles washes out his bloodstained garments and then writes Sarah a long, somewhat stilted but nevertheless sincere, letter. He gives the letter to Sam to deliver. He plans to go to Lyme and break his engagement with Ernestina, and then return to Exeter for Sarah.

Upon returning to Lyme, Charles goes to Ernestina and tries to tell her that he is unworthy of her. He tells her that he proposed to her with something less than honorable intentions, and that her position as the only child of a wealthy merchant influenced him. She is shocked, but instinctively refuses to accept this statement. Ernestina wavers between strength and weakness in her reaction to the news. Her outrage is more than a personal reaction, for marriage is an important institution in itself, as far as women are concerned, and Ernestina feels threatened by this change in her prospects. The breaking of an engagement is a more profound blow to such a woman than it would be to her modern counterpart, as evidenced by her threat of legal action against Charles to protect her reputation. But at last she weakens and begs Charles to remain. She tells him that she realizes he thinks that she is immature, but she knows that she will change. She says that he feels he is unworthy because he lacks confidence in himself, and she wants to devote herself to helping him.

Charles is deeply touched by what she has said, but as a result, he finds himself forced to admit the real cause of the broken engagement. He finally admits that he is in love with another, though he does not reveal her name. Angry at first, Ernestina gives way to despair and apparently faints. Although her pain is real, Charles notices that the fainting spell is a bit too perfect to be real and is not as shocked by it as one might imagine. It is simply a conventional gesture, a way in which a young lady could express outrage and shock, since screaming, tearing one's hair, or attacking someone else are not acceptable gestures. Charles summons the maid to attend her while he goes to fetch Dr. Grogan.

Charles returns to his rooms at the hotel after telling Dr. Grogan what has occurred. The doctor is nearly as shocked as was Ernestina, for an action such as this was less common and less accepted than it was to become later on. Charles feels like a traitor, but resigns himself to the consequences of his act. Sam comes to Charles shortly and asks him if it is true that he has terminated his engagement to Ernestina, and Charles confirms that it is. Sam is more disturbed about his own future than that of his fiancée's mistress, and questions Charles about his own prospects. In his distraught state, Charles is unable to give Sam a coherent or concrete answer to his questions, which Sam interprets as indifference. Frustrated and angry, Sam resigns.

Here Fowles hints that Sam's rebellious attitude towards Charles isn't the only misbehavior Sam is guilty of. As we shall see later, Sam has been looking out for his own interests ever since he knew that Charles would probably not inherit much money from his uncle.

Caught up in the emotion created by the events, Charles is hardly less amazed and shocked by what is happening than are the others. But he consoles himself that he will return to Sarah as soon as he can. In the meantime, he drafts a letter to Ernestina's father, and while he is writing, the doctor returns.

While Charles and Sam are arguing at the hotel, Aunt Tranter returns home to find Dr. Grogan there and the house in an uproar. She confers with Dr. Grogan, who has given Ernestina something to make her sleep. Then Mary tearfully explains to her what has happened, not failing to include that Sam has left Charles' employ because, Mary says, of his former master's treatment of Ernestina. Thus part of Mary's unhappiness is based on her fears for herself and Sam. Aunt Tranter promises her that the two of them will be taken care of, and Mary joyfully runs to Sam in the back of the house, where he has been waiting for her since his return from talking with Charles.

The scene then shifts back to Charles and Dr. Grogan. The doctor has just returned from taking care of Ernestina. He sharply lectures Charles on the vileness of his act, but also offers a bit of consolation as a friend. He states that Charles must try to become a better person in order to mitigate some of the damage he has just done. If he does not, then the harm already done will only be made worse, for it will have served no purpose. Leaving Charles with this odd bit of advice, he wishes him good luck, and warns him to be out of town within the hour.

Charles returns to Exeter, only to find that Sarah has disappeared without leaving an address where she might be found. After checking at her hotel, Charles discovers that Sam never delivered the letter to Sarah. He is both angry and helpless since there is nothing he can do about it now. He vows to find Sarah and boards a train, intending to go to London and locate her. He hopes to have a compartment to himself; however, at the last moment, a bearded stranger also boards the train. Both men exchange disapproving glances, and the journey begins. Though Charles is unaware of the fact, the reader is informed that this stranger is the *persona* of John Fowles. And in this chapter the author attempts to explain how he will conclude the novel.

In this fanciful encounter with one of his characters, Fowles illustrates some of the problems of writing a novel. He stares at Charles, who has fallen asleep, and like some minor deity, wonders what to do with him. At this point neither Charles nor Fowles know where Sarah is, so neither is of any help. Fowles disgresses and explains the art of novel writing as pitting the characters and their desires against one another, letting them fight it out and describing the fight. But while the fight is in progress, the novelist has already decided who will win in advance. He is a good novelist if his audience does not guess the victor before he chooses to tell them.

But Fowles has decided to challenge this convention; he has decided to let these characters, Charles and Sarah, decide the fight for themselves, or so he says. In order to accomplish this, he will provide two endings, one in which Charles wins and one in which Sarah does. The reader might note here that both the charm and difficulty of the novel lie in the fact that it has two endings, for it is difficult not to perceive one as true and the other as false. If we follow Fowles' hint in this chapter, they both are simply possible endings for a novel we have just observed unfold. However, we might also notice that the first conclusion is the one we might perhaps expect to find in such a novel, while the second has far less of that conclusiveness which Fowles indicates is desirable in such a novel. He is tempted, he says, to end it right here, with Charles riding into London on the train, but the conventions of the novel do not allow for such an inconclusive ending.

Chapters 56-61

Charles engages detectives to look for Sarah, but they fail. In the meantime, he receives a letter from Mr. Freeman, delivered by his solicitor, requesting that he attend a meeting with Freeman and his solicitors if he wishes to avoid facing an action in a suit for a breach of the engagement contract. Charles consults with his solicitor and friend, a Mr. Montague, who informs him that this letter, while unpleasant, is a stroke of luck. Montague tells Charles that he will probably have to admit publicly to having been dishonorable in his relations with the Freemans, but that such an admission is far better than having to defend himself in a lawsuit.

At the humiliating meeting which Charles and Montague attend, Charles consents to sign a document in which he fully admits his guilt in his breach of contract for marriage to Ernestina. The terms of the admission, it might be noted, emphasize that marriage had its economic, as well as its social aspects, and hence could well be considered to be a sort of contract. After this, Charles continues to search for Sarah in London but ultimately gives up. Upon Montague's advice, he decides to travel abroad for awhile.

Twenty months pass, and we discover that Mary and Sam are living in London and that Mary is expecting her second child. Currently she is strolling in a park and enjoying the early spring weather. However, she is soon surprised by the sight of Sarah Woodruff alighting from a carriage not far from her. She tells Sam of the surprising sight, and he is rather more disturbed by the news than one would think likely. His distress is at least partly due to his sense of guilt over the role he played in destroying the relationship that existed between Sarah and his former master, Charles, even though he still disapproves of Charles' actions.

The rest of this chapter describes the young couple's life in London and their rise from the servant class. Sam is now a successful employee at Mr. Freeman's haberdashery and is gaining the experience which he hopes someday to use in establishing his own business. Although Sam has accepted his good fortune with equanimity, Mary is still amazed by the fact that she is married to a man who is so successful that she can even afford to hire a young girl to be their maid, a job she herself had only a short time before.

Charles travels throughout Europe and the Mediterranean countries, but he is affected little by his experiences. He keeps a journal of the daily events of his travels, but expresses his actual feelings only in poetry which he shows to no one. Fowles quotes the entirety of Matthew Arnold's poem "To Marguerite" as expressing some of Charles' feelings about his isolation and loneliness better than Charles himself could.

However, Charles eventually begins to feel that perhaps the Sarah whom he longs for never really existed except as an ideal, that perhaps the real woman did not match the image he created and has carried with him all these months. Although he does not despair of ever finding her again, somehow the need to find her becomes less urgent.

After meeting a charming pair of Americans, an elderly man and his nephew, Charles decides to visit America. His view of himself as a rebel and outcast no doubt contribute to his desire to visit America, a country so unlike and yet so like his home. In this chapter, Fowles raises the question of why Charles does not completely give in to despair over his loss and disgrace and perhaps commit suicide. But he answers his own question with the suggestion that Charles has found some comfort in the knowledge that he is an outcast and thus different from others of his kind. Then, too, when he encounters young couples on his travels, he cannot say that he feels envy for them, but only relief that he did not give in to convention and consummate a matter that was false. This is small comfort, in the face of his loss, but apparently it sustains him for the time.

In Chapter 59, Fowles describes Charles' travels in America. We get a very brief glimpse of the United States of this period as compared to England. Here, while the influence of England is strong, it is tempered by the different problems faced by the struggling country that was still recovering from the devastation of the Civil War. Charles is impressed by the vitality of the country and the openness of its people, but he swiftly books the first passage to Europe when Montague sends a cable that Sarah Woodruff has been located in London. After some twenty months of separation, she still has a powerful effect on him.

In Chapter 60, we read the first of two possible endings to the story. In this version, Sarah is found residing in London under the name of Mrs. Roughwood. Charles believes her to be employed as a governess for a family, but it turns out that she is an assistant and an artist's model for Mr. Rossetti, a well-known artist whose work is considered somewhat shocking by many Victorians.

In spite of Montague's advice, Charles goes to see Sarah. He is surprised to find that she does not need someone to rescue her from penury or immorality, for his greatest fear was that he would find her living a miserable existence as an underpaid governess, or even worse, as a prostitute. However, his expectations are contradicted by the confident, well-dressed young woman Sarah has become.

We quickly perceive the contrast between Sarah's world of new trends and ideas and Ernestina's world, in which old values still hold sway, even when they are questioned. Charles finds himself caught between them; he finds Sarah's new life rather uncomfortably bohemian for his tastes, yet he cannot help admiring her strength and freedom, qualities he admired in the Americans whom he recently met.

Sarah is not to be won easily though. She refuses to marry Charles, and when he asks her why, she obliquely states that she simply wishes *not* to marry, something, she says, he will never understand. Her life, as it is, is pleasant and is all that she wants.

Charles is stunned when she admits that she saw his advertisements inquiring about her and that she moved and changed her name because of them. He is ready to leave, despairing that she ever loved him when she begs him to stay long enough to meet someone, a "lady" who will explain her motives to him. He is puzzled but waits. Sarah leaves, and shortly another young woman enters and places a child on the floor. Charles asks her where the "lady" is, and she points at the child. Rather dramatically, Charles realizes that it is his and Sarah's child. Sarah comes back a few moments later, and they embrace. Whether or not they will ever marry is not certain, but the story ends with the couple finally united, and with their love strengthened by all they have gone through.

This ending fulfills the romantic convention in which the lovers are finally united after a long period of trials and separations.

Although this ending may be a conventional ending for many Victorian novels, it is deceptively so, for there is something quite modern in the manner in which the lovers are reconciled. Furthermore, this ending does not meet the criteria for most love stories—that is, that they have a fairly well-defined conclusion, whether it be happy or tragic. The story could end here, but Fowles is dissatisfied and has his characters perform their parts again, with different results.

In Chapter 61, Fowles intrudes for the last time, posing as a sort of theater director who takes great pleasure in manipulating his characters to achieve different roles. Fowles has just finished observing and directing the scene between Sarah and Charles in Dante Gabriel Rossetti's house and seems quite amused by it. He steps into a coach and leaves, after first setting his watch back a quarter of an hour. We are told this is an affectation of his, but, as we shall see, since the observer is the author, he has in fact turned back time.

We return to the scene in Rossetti's house, but we are back at the point where Charles believes he has been betrayed. Now, instead of denying that she has betrayed him, and finally admitting that she loves him, Sarah admits nothing; she remains as silent and enigmatic as ever. And again, utterly disgusted with himself and with the woman he allowed himself to fall in love with, Charles leaves. He sees the child in the arms of a young woman as he exits but takes no further notice of it.

He leaves, bitter and alienated, to search for a new life for himself. The narrator returns and explains that his intervention in this story has no more effect than the random particle of radiation that causes a mutation in some evolving organism, one that may, perhaps, contribute to its survival. Thus Charles and Sarah both face the world alone, as someday their child must also do.

However, Fowles' final choice of a conclusion is not as random as he would make it seem. In discovering that he could reject conventional attitudes, and love Sarah regardless of the social consequences, Charles discovered a strength in himself that he did not have before. Fowles could have ended the novel there, with the couple reunited. But just as he worked within the conventions of the novel before, he rejects them now, and arrives at a conclusion where there are no lovers, only individual people.

Although Fowles offers us two "endings," they both move the reader towards this final conclusion. Fowles has differed from most authors in that he has revealed to his audience the process, the alternatives, as well as the final result, but it was towards this final result that the characters were moving all along.

Structure, Style, and Technique

In *The French Lieutenant's Woman,* John Fowles does not merely recreate a Victorian novel; neither does he parody one. He does a little of both, but also much more. The subject of this novel is essentially the same as that of his other works: the relationship between life and art, the artist and his creation, and the isolation resulting from an individual's struggle for selfhood. He works within the tradition of the Victorian novel and consciously uses its conventions to serve his own design, all the while carefully informing the reader exactly what he is doing. His style purposely combines a flowing nineteenth-century prose style with an anachronistic twentieth-century perspective.

Fowles is as concerned with the details of the setting as were his Victorian counterparts. But he is also conscious that he is setting a scene and does not hesitate to intrude into the narrative himself in order to show the reader how he manipulates reality through his art. Like Dickens, Fowles uses dialogue to reveal the personalities of his characters and often he will satirize them as well. For example, Charles' attitudes toward Sarah and Ernestina are revealed in the way he talks to them. He is forever uncomfortable with Sarah because she won't accept the way in which he categorizes the world, including his view of her. Sarah's responses to the world around her, as seen through her words and actions are consistent, for she is already aware of herself as an individual who cannot be defined by conventional roles. However, Charles changes, depending upon whom he talks to, because he really does not know who he is yet, and he sees himself as playing a series of roles. With his fiancée, he is indulgent and paternal; with his servant Sam, he is patronizing and humorous at Sam's expense, and with Sarah, he is stiff and uncomfortable. When he attempts to respond to Sarah's honesty, he hears the hollowness of his own conventional responses.

Fowles does not recreate his Victorian world uncritically. He focuses on those aspects of the Victorian era that would seem most alien to a modern reader. In particular, he is concerned with Victorian attitudes towards women, economics, science, and philosophy. In this romance, Fowles examines the problems of two socially and economically oppressed groups in nineteenth-century England: the poverty of the working and servant classes, and the economic and social entrapment of women. While the plot traces a love story, or what seems to be a love story, the reader questions what sort of love existed in a society where many marriages were based as much on economics as on love. This story is thus not really a romance at all, for Fowles' objective is not to unite his two protagonists, Sarah and Charles, but to show what each human being must face in life in order to be able to grow.

While Fowles has titled his book *The French Lieutenant's Woman*, Sarah Woodruff is not really the central character. She does not change greatly in the novel as it progresses, for she has already arrived at an awareness that she must go beyond the definition of her individuality that society has imposed upon her. Because her situation was intolerable, she was forced to see through it and beyond it in order to find meaning and some sort of happiness in her life. In the early chapters of the novel, she perhaps makes one last effort to establish a life within the norms of Victorian society. She chooses the role of the outcast, "the French lieutenant's whore," and also falls in love with Charles or causes him to fall in love with her. But even as she draws Charles away from his unquestioning acceptance of his life, she finds that she does not want to be rescued from her plight. She has already rescued herself.

Charles, it seems, is the actual protagonist of this novel, for he must travel from ignorance to understanding, by following the woman whom he thinks he is helping, but who in fact is his mentor. He must discard each layer of the false Charles: Charles the naturalist, Charles the gentleman, Charles the rake, and perhaps even Charles the lover, in order to find Charles the human being. The knowledge he arrives at is bitter, for he has lost all his illusions, as Sarah discarded hers sometime before. But the result itself is not bitter. Although Charles and Sarah are not reunited, for life's answers are never as simple and perfect as those of art, they both achieve a maturity that enables them to control their lives as long as they remember to look for answers nowhere but in themselves.

Fowles has taken two traditional romantic characters, a young hero and a mysterious woman, and has transformed them into human beings.

There is no French lieutenant to pine after, and Sarah's life is not a tragedy that echoes her nickname in Lyme. Charles' gift of marriage is not a gift at all. While the novel could have ended with the couple's reconciliation, as it might have had it been a traditional romance, Fowles does not end it there. In the second ending, Sarah rejects the familiar security that Charles offers and both are forced to go on alone.

Fowles' novel echoes the doubts raised by such novelists as Thomas Hardy, and by such poets as Matthew Arnold and Alfred Lord Tennyson, about the solidity of the Victorian view of the world. The world was changing and old standards no longer applied, though they lingered on long after many had discarded them in their hearts. This theme that was approached by writers in the nineteenth century is picked up again by Fowles and carried to a logical conclusion. The novel is therefore actually a psychological study of an individual rather than a romance. It is a novel of individual growth and the awareness of one's basic isolation which accompanies that growth.

List of Characters

SARAH WOODRUFF

She is an educated but impoverished young woman. She is called "the French Lieutenant's Woman" or "Tragedy" or "the French lieutenant's whore" because it is believed that she had an affair with a shipwrecked French sailor. It is also believed that she is half mad with grief and that she stares out to sea, vainly hoping for the day he will return to her. Because of her reputation she can no longer gain any employment until Mrs. Poulteney hires her as a paid companion. Sarah is a mysterious figure. No one knows much about her, and later we find that much of what people believe about her is untrue.

CHARLES SMITHSON

He is a wealthy gentleman and is heir to a minor title. His hobby is collecting fossils and he considers himself to be something of a naturalist. He is an admirer of the controversial Darwin and he is rather pleased with himself that he is one of a minority in the 1860s to hold scientifically advanced ideas, such as the theories espoused by Darwin and others. He is both sensitive and intelligent, but he is unsure of himself. He is bored and dissatisfied with the course his life is taking. His fiancée is Ernestina Freeman, but that relationship is changed when he meets Sarah Woodruff.

ERNESTINA FREEMAN

Ernestina is Charles' fiancée. She is attractive and clever but also very young and naive. Although she considers herself to be a modern young woman, her attitudes are similar, for the most part, to those of most proper young ladies. She is vacationing in Lyme when the story opens, staying with Aunt Tranter.

AUNT TRANTER

Ernestina's aunt is a kindly woman whose temperament contrasts greatly with that of the sharp-tongued Mrs. Poulteney. Aunt Tranter's honesty and lack of hypocrisy seem to present a welcome bright spot in the small town governed by the malicious gossip of less charitable souls.

MRS. POULTENEY

The vicar convinces the wealthy widow to take in Sarah Woodruff and give her employment. Mrs. Poulteney's main motive in doing so is to show how charitable she is, and it does not stem from any real feelings of compassion for Sarah. Mrs. Poulteney is a stereotype, a conglomerate of all the malicious old villainesses who have appeared in numerous Victorian novels.

DR. GROGAN

He is a friendly man whom Charles finds to be a sympathetic listener. Although he feels sorry for Sarah Woodruff, unlike Charles, he cannot take her seriously. He tries to convince Charles that she really is ill. Dr. Grogan, like Aunt Tranter, represents a type of Victorian character who seems more understanding and less hampered by convention than most people. Part of the reason for this is that both of the older people actually belong to the generation before Victoria's, an era somewhat less repressive in certain respects.

CAPTAIN AND MRS. TALBOT

Sarah was the governess for the Talbot's children when she met the French lieutenant. Even after she told them of her experience with him, they did not condemn her for it.

LIEUTENANT VARGUENNES

Caught in a shipwreck, his leg was injured, and Varguennes was nursed at the home of the Talbots, mostly by Sarah. Although he flirted with Sarah, and wished to seduce her, he was married, as she later found out.

MRS. FAIRLEY

She is Mrs. Poulteney's housekeeper and is as unkind as her mistress. She delights in spying on Sarah and reporting her activities to Mrs. Poulteney.

MILLIE

Mrs. Poulteney's young maid who is befriended by Sarah.

MARY

Aunt Tranter's maid whose life is considerably more pleasant than Millie's. She eventually marries Charles' man-servant, Sam Farrow.

SAM FARROW

While Sam is often the object of Charles' teasing, he is not merely a humorous figure as was Dickens' Sam Weller. He takes himself seriously and is an ambitious member of the working class. He is determined to wed Mary and make a good life for the two of them.

SIR ROBERT

Charles Smithson's uncle. It is his title that Charles hopes to inherit, although that prospect is altered when Sir Robert marries Mrs. Tomkins, an attractive widow.

LIEUTENANT DE LÁ RONCIÈRE and MARIE DE MORELL

These are two individuals in a case history given to Charles by Dr. Grogan for him to read. The doctor hopes that reading about how the neurotic young woman convinced the French courts that she had been assaulted and her family sent poison-pen letters by the officer would convince Charles that Sarah possibly had similar intentions regarding him. While Charles conceded that the story might be true, he did not believe it applied to Sarah.

MR. FREEMAN

He was a haberdasher who became very successful. One sign of his success was that he, a member of the middle class, could have his daughter marry one of the nobility.

GABRIEL AND CHRISTINA ROSSETTI

They were the founders of a school of art called the Pre-Raphaelite school. In their day they were considered as radical as Mr. Freeman was conservative. However, by the time Sarah came to stay with them, their work, while still shocking to some, was coming to be more accepted.

JOHN FOWLES

He is the bearded man who enters the novel several times as an observer and sometimes as a sort of theatrical director. He comments on the actions of his characters and discusses the relationship between the art of the novel and life.

Study Questions

1. Compare the characters of Sarah and Ernestina. In what ways are they affected by Victorian attitudes towards women? In what ways do their different social and economic status affect their experiences?
2. Compare the lives of Sam, Mary, and other members of the working class with those of their employers. What social attitudes do they have? In what ways do their attitudes diverge?
3. Discuss Charles. In what ways does he avoid learning about who he

is? For example, discuss his interest in paleontology or his desire to help Sarah.

4. Why does Charles decide to go to the brothel and then change his mind? Compare this with his experience with the prostitute Sarah. What do his reactions mean? Discuss whether it would be possible for a man to idealize some women, while he might feel no guilt about exploiting others. What attitudes towards women would this foster?

5. Why does Fowles give the novel two conclusions? Do you consider them to be equally viable options, or is one more of a conclusion than the other?

6. How is Charles changed by his romance with Sarah? Is it a change for the better or for the worse?

7. Why does Sarah allow herself to be called "the French lieutenant's whore" when in fact she never had sex with him? Why in fact did she start the rumor at all, since she was the one who first mentioned it to her employer, Mrs. Talbot?

8. Compare this novel with a popular romance or a gothic novel, either of the nineteenth century or the present. What conventions of these novels does Fowles adopt? What does he change or discard?

9. Compare this novel with a novel by Thomas Hardy, George Eliot, or Charles Dickens.

10. Discuss the two long poems quoted from by Fowles in his novel.

11. Read the other poems referred to in the opening quotations. What light, if any, do they throw on your understanding of either the novel or Victorian attitudes towards life.

12. Is Fowles too one-sided in his description of people in the nineteenth century? Discuss.

13. What is Fowles saying about the novel as an art form? Does he practice what he preaches?

14. Read Fowles' *The Collector* and *The Magus*. Are their themes and characters similar in spite of differences in plot and setting? Discuss.

Selected Bibliography

Palmer, William J. *The Fiction of John Fowles: Tradition, Art, and the Loneliness of Selfhood*. Columbia: University of Missouri Press, 1974.

Wolfe, Peter. *John Fowles: Magus or Moralist?* Lewisburg: Bucknell University Press, 1976.

NOTES

NOTES

NOTES

NOTES

NOTES